MARTIAL ARTS for Kids

A LOOK AT KARATE

Cara Krenn

Lerner Publications ◆ Minneapolis

Lerner Publications Company
An imprint of Lerner Publishing Group, Inc.
241 First Avenue North
Minneapolis, MN 55401 USA

For reading levels and more information, look up this title at www.lernerbooks.com.

Main body text set in Mikado.
Typeface provided by HVD.

Editor: Annie Zheng **Designer:** Mary Ross

Library of Congress Cataloging-in-Publication Data

Names: Krenn, Cara, author.
Title: A look at karate / Cara Krenn.
Description: Minneapolis, MN : Lerner Publications, [2025] | Series: Lerner sports rookie. Martial arts for kids | Includes bibliographical references and index. | Audience: Ages 5–8 | Audience: Grades K–1 | Summary: "Players block, punch, and kick their way into karate! Young readers will learn more about how the sport works, what lessons look like, what types of contests there are, and more"— Provided by publisher.
Identifiers: LCCN 2024009015 (print) | LCCN 2024009016 (ebook) | ISBN 9798765647974 (library binding) | ISBN 9798765662083 (paperback) | ISBN 9798765656235 (epub)
Subjects: LCSH: Karate—Juvenile literature.
Classification: LCC GV1114.3 .K74 2025 (print) | LCC GV1114.3 (ebook) | DDC 796.815/3—dc23/eng/20240320

LC record available at https://lccn.loc.gov/2024009015
LC ebook record available at https://lccn.loc.gov/2024009016

Manufactured in the United States of America
1-1011022-53358-6/26/2024

Table of Contents

CHAPTER 1

What Is Karate?

Punch. Block. Strike. It's time for karate!

Karate is a popular sport. Students learn how to defend themselves and block moves!

Karate students use their whole body. They may use their hands, feet, knees, and elbows to strike an opponent.

FUN FACT

Karate began on the Japanese islands of Okinawa.

CHAPTER 2

Karate Basics

Karate students wear a uniform. They wear pants, a jacket, and a belt. The belt color shows your rank. Belts range from white to black.

Karate students show respect by bowing. They bow to their teacher and one another.

FUN FACT

A karate school is called a dojo.

CHAPTER 3

What to Expect

During lessons, students practice moves against a pad. Students may also practice moves with another person in a spar.

FUN FACT

Karate students can learn to break a wood board with their hand!

Teachers help guide students through new moves.

UP CLOSE!
Basic Karate Punch

Stand with your feet apart. Make fists with your hands. Keep one fist at your side. Then punch your other fist straight out in front of you, with your palm facing down.

CHAPTER 4

Karate Superstar

Karate has many types of contests. Kumite is fighting another person. You earn points for punches and kicks.

FUN FACT

Olympic kumite limits hits to keep people safe.

In kata, you perform a series of moves alone. Judges award points for your moves.

Karate is fun and exciting.
Are you ready to try it?

Glossary

opponent: a player you compete against

rank: level of skill

spar: a practice fight

strike: to hit

Learn More

Peters, Katie. *Karate: A First Look*. Minneapolis: Lerner Publications, 2023.
Sterling, Holly. *Karate Kids*. Somerville, MA: Candlewick, 2020.
Vink, Amanda. *Karate*. New York: PowerKids, 2020.

Index

Photo Acknowledgments

Image credits: Phynart Studio/Getty Images, p. 5; wsfurlan/Getty Images, p. 7; Frazao Studio Latino/Getty Images, p. 9; FatCamera/Getty Images, pp. 11, 23; PeopleImages/Getty Images, p. 13; JGI/Tom Grill/Getty Images, p. 15; Stefan Tomic/Getty Images, pp. 16, 21; FOTOGRAFIA INC./Getty Images, p. 17; The Asahi Shimbun via Getty Images, p. 19. Design elements: str33tcat/Getty Images; ulimi/Getty Images; Tuomas A. Lehtinen/Getty Images.
Cover: Phynart Studio/Getty Images.